DO-IT-TOGETHER SCREEN PRINTING

BY JOHN ISAACSON

DO-IT-YOURSELF SCREENPRINTING

AN INSTRUCTIONAL GRAPHIC NOVEL
PART I:
"HOW TO TURN YOUR HOME INTO A T-SHIRT FACTORY"
PART II:
"TRIAL AND TRIBULATION ON TELEGRAPH AVENUE"
PART III:

"DREAM JOB OR NIGHTMARE JOB?"

BY JOHN ISAACSON

ISBN 978-0-9770557-4-6
THIS IS MICROCOSM # 76034

FIRST PRINTING 5,000 COPIES 12/1/7
SECOND PRINTING 5,000 COPIES 4/1/11

MICROCOSM PUBLISHING
222 S. ROGERS ST.
BLOOMINGTON, IN. 47404

PO BOX 14332
PORTLAND, OR 97293

www.microcosmpublishing.com

MORE JOHN ISAACSON AT:
www.unlay.com

DIY SCREENPRINTING

IN ORDER TO PRINT T-SHIRTS IN THE COMFORT OF YOUR OWN HOME, YOU MUST PROCURE A SILKSCREEN

3

Glass (top)

Transparency (under glass)

Emulsion-coated screen hardening under light exposure

Screen frame

18 × 20

KEEP AN EYE ON THE CLOCK!.!.!.

Black paper

SPEEDBALL SCREEN PRINTING SYSTEM RECOMMENDED EXPOSURE CHART

150 Watt Bulb Screen Size	150 Watt Bulb Height	Exposure Time
8 x 10	12 inches	45 minutes
10 x 14	12 inches	45 minutes
12 x 18	15 inches	1 hr. 14 min.
16 x 20	17 inches	1 hr. 32 min.
18 x 20	17 inches	1 hr. 32 min.

SET AN ALARM!!!

NOTES ON TRANSPARENCIES

DO NOT use gray-scale images; use ONLY black and white images (half tones or bit-maps). Set copier on maximum darkness to get a thick layer of toner.

Eventually the emulsion that was <u>NOT</u> <u>exposed</u> to light (i.e. under the dark parts of the trans-parency) will <u>wash out</u> of the screen.

Hold it up to a light source to check that all the emulsion has washed out.

10

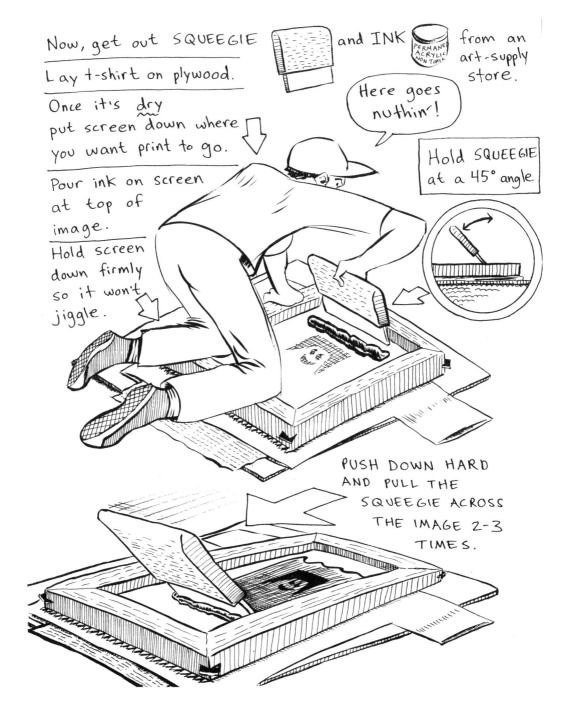

Now, get out SQUEEGIE and INK from an art-supply store.

Lay t-shirt on plywood.

Once it's dry put screen down where you want print to go.

Pour ink on screen at top of image.

Hold screen down firmly so it won't jiggle.

PERMANENT ACRYLIC NON TOXIC

Here goes nuthin'!

Hold SQUEEGIE at a 45° angle

PUSH DOWN HARD AND PULL THE SQUEEGIE ACROSS THE IMAGE 2-3 TIMES.

11

12

Continue exercise while walking up stairs...
End result: Silkscreen is all dry and ready to print with a new color ink

Ooh— I think I'll try purple or green!

My arms are tired though!

15

ORDER AN EXPURTLY SILKSCREENED-BY-HAND T-SHIRT TODAY!!!

SCREENPRINTER PROFILE: TAYLOR MADE

What inspired you to start screen-printing?
My interest in screenprinting came about when I started to get really inspired to decorate my clothing. I was trying hard with yucky iron-ons. I ran into a few local people who were screenprinting and designing clothes themselves and they kinda led me in the right direction.

What type of surfaces do you print on?
Clothing and fabric mostly.

What types of ink do you use?
I started with water based Versatex ink (for paper and fabric), but when I had access to a dryer I switched to Plastisol. Union ink is good, but I'm not too picky about brands.

What size print runs do you do? (100's - 10's?)
Probably between 10-20. I have to use a flash dryer instead of a conveyor belt dryer now, so it's more time consuming and more boring (you just have to wait there while it cures). Plus, I want to stay away from mass-production.

How many colors do you generally use per design?
Although I have a 6-color press, I usually just use 2 screens and 2 colors per design. But I also really like to do blends of many colors on one screen.

How do you separate and register colors? (on a computer - photoshop - illustrator / by hand with sharpie and vellum / with stencils)
I started with drawing ink and vellum, but then soon switched to using Photoshop. I recently returned to using ink and it's a lot of fun.

How do you protect yourself from toxic materials such as inks and solvents while printing / cleaning up?
Um, not very well. I work in a well ventilated studio. I just bought a respirator from Home Depot to wear when things are getting stinky though. I don't usually wear gloves, but maybe I should. I keep hearing different things about the safety of the products I use, so perhaps I should be more careful than I am.

Where do you print?
In my garage. Sometimes at my old work.

What do you listen to while you print?
My ipod, because it's portable. Depends what mood I'm in. I kinda like to print to music that makes you wanna dance, because then I can dance while I'm waiting for my ink to cure.

Where can we see your work?
My website (www.taylormadeclothes.com). Shops that carry handmade items, like my collective, Rock Paper Scissors (www.rpscollective.com).

19

HEY THERE! THANKS FOR TAKING AN INTEREST IN "DO-IT-YOURSELF SILKSCREEN"

SEVERAL REVIEWS AND LETTERS HAVE PROMPTED ME TO INCLUDE THIS **INSERT** TO THE COMIC

THANK YOU FOR THOUGHT-FUL REVIEWS HeartattaCK, RAZORCAKE,

I Heart attack

INTRO TO THE INSERT

FIRST OF ALL, THIS COMIC IS **NOT** INTENDED TO BE USED AS A SINGLE SOURCE OF INFORMATION ABOUT SILKSCREENING

THE INK DRIED IN MY SCREEN! YOU JERK!

LIAR!

INSTEAD, THIS COMIC **IS** INTENDED TO BE USED AS A VISUAL COMPLEMENT TO THE INSTRUCTION BOOKLET INCLUDED IN THE **DIAZO PHOTO EMULSION KIT** MADE BY SPEED BALL SCREEN-PRINTING * (OR ANY OTHER INSTRUCTION MANUAL

EMULSION | KIT | SENSITIZER | INSTRUCTIONS

THIS INSERT INCLUDES INFORMATION ABOUT:
- TRANSPARENCIES
- PHOTO EMULSION
- MESH COUNTS
- CURING & CLEANING
- A SUPPLY LIST
- ON-LINE RESOURCES

LOOK FOR UPCOMING ISSUES OF "DO-IT-YOUR-SELF SILKSCREENG"

(#2) "HOW TO SELL YOUR T-SHIRTS ON THE STREET"

(#3) "WORKING IN A T-SHIRT FACTORY"

* www.speedballart.com

20

TRANSPARENCIES

1) YOUR ORIGINAL ARTWORK YOU WANT TO PUT ON A T-SHIRT:

LOOKIT MY PIXSTCHURE!

NO GRAY!

ONLY BLACK!

AND WHITE

2) YOU CAN GET TRANSPARENCIES AT A COPY STORE (LIKE KINKO'S)

TWO TRANS-PARENCIES PLEASE!

AGAIN?

3) WHAT IS A TRANSPARENCY? A TRANSPARENCY IS A CLEAR PLASTIC 8½ × 11" SHEET. YOU'VE PROBABLY SEEN THEM USED BEFORE ON OVERHEAD PROJECTORS

OH! I CAN SEE THRU

4) IT GOES IN THE COPIER THROUGH THE BYPASS TRAY

YOU KNOW HOW TO USE A COPIER, RIGHT?

* ALWAYS RUN A TEST COPY FIRST!

YOU FLIP DOWN ON THE SIDE OF THE COPIER

JERK

5) USE THE "LIGHTEN/DARKEN" FEATURE ON THE COPY MACHINE TO MAKE THE **TONER** (i.e. black stuff) ON THE COPY AS THICK AS POSSIBLE

JOIN THE DARK SIDE!

RESET START

NO COPIES 1

DARKEN LIGHTEN

6) LINE UP _TWO_ TRANSPARENCIES OF YOUR IMAGE AND THEN HOLD THEM UP TO THE LIGHT, TO MAKE SURE THAT _NO_ LIGHT IS GETTING THROUGH THE BLACK PARTS.

tape them together

PHOTO EMULSION

I RECOMMEND USING THE **DIAZO PHOTO EMULSION KIT** (This includes both emulsion, sensitizer, AND INSTRUCTIONS) available from Speedball screen printing.
www.speedballart.com

DIFFERENT TYPES OF PHOTO EMULSION ARE MADE FOR PRINTING WITH EACH TYPE OF INK.
EACH TYPE OF INK IS MADE FOR PRINTING ON (AND ADHERING TO) DIFFERENT TYPES OF SURFACES, OR "SUBSTRATES".

You can search by "ink" and "substrates" at:
www.nazdar.com OR www.unionink.com

You can order products from both these sites at:
www.midwestsignandscreen.com
AND
www.creativescreentech.com

You should buy t-shirts at www.americanapparel.net OR YOUR LOCAL THRIFT STORE

Look at your local library for books about screen printing.

MESH COUNT

THESE NUMBERS ARE THE SCREEN'S **MESH COUNT**

Q: WHAT IS MESH COUNT? **A:** MESH COUNT IS THE NUMBER OF <u>THREADS PER INCH</u> IN A SILK SCREEN

> THE MORE THREADS PER INCH, THE TIGHTER THE WEAVE. THE TIGHTER THE WEAVE, THE LESS INK GETS THROUGH THE SCREEN. **DARK-COLORED** FABRICS NEED A THICK LAYER OF INK (LOW MESH COUNT). **LIGHT-COLORED** FABRICS ONLY NEED A THIN LAYER OF INK (HIGHER MESH COUNT)

LOOSER MESH		MEDIUM MESH	TIGHT MESH	
83 Threads per inch	**110** Threads per inch	**156** Threads per inch	**195** Threads per inch	**305** Threads per inch
LOTS OF INK COMES THROUGH			LESS INK COMES THROUGH	
IDEAL FOR PRINTING MAXOPAKE WHITE OR OTHER LIGHT COLORED INKS WHICH TEND TO BE THICKER ON TO **DARK** COLORED FABRICS	PRETTY STANDARD USED FOR PRINTING MAXOPAKE LIGHT **OR** DARK INKS ON TO **LIGHT** COLORED FABRIC	GOOD FOR PRINTING DESIGNS WITH LOTS OF TINY DETAIL USING THINNER, DARKER, ULTRASOFT INKS ON TO **LIGHT-COLORED FABRIC**	COMMONLY USED FOR PRINTING WITH WATER-BASED INK ON TO PAPER	USED TO GET SUPER FINE DETAIL (LIKE HALF-TONES) USING PROCESS (CMYK) COLORS ON TO **LIGHT COLORED FABRIC**

> Source: www.ryanrss.com

SUPPLY LIST

THESE ITEMS ARE AVAILABLE AT: www.creativescreentech.com

① PHOTO EMULSION

SPEED BALL SCREEN PRINTING DIAZO PHOTO EMULSION KIT

INSTRUCTIONS
SENSITIZER
EMULSION

SPEEDBALL

PHOTO EMULS.

OR

PRE-MIXED QUART OF PHOTO EMULSION

*STORE THIS STUFF IN A DARK PLACE

② SOMETHING TO COAT SCREENS WITH: EITHER

Ⓐ STRAIGHT-EDGED (MACHINE-CUT, LIKE, FROM A BOX) PIECE OF CARDBOARD

FOR COATING SCREEN WITH EMULSION

OR YOU CAN USE AN "EMULSION COATER" AVAILABLE AT Creative Screen Tech.

*USUALLY FOUND IN T-SHIRT PRINTING SHOPS OR COLLEGE ART CLASSES.

③ SILK SCREENS: WOODEN FRAMES BOUGHT PRE-ASSEMBLED OR IN PIECES FROM YOUR LOCAL ART STORE. MESH AND STAPLE GUN MAY BE NECESSARY

OR

ALUMINUM FRAMES: ORDER FROM CREATIVE SCREEN OR MIDWEST SUPPLY - sizes and mesh counts vary

④ SQUEEGIE - sizes vary, again

NOT LIKE A SQUEEGIE FOR WASHING YOUR WINDOWSHEILD!

RUBBER DENSITY VARIES: firm - medium - soft

(5) WATER, HOSE, PRESSURE-BLASTER, OR MINERAL SPIRITS FOR CLEANING UP INK.

MINERAL SPIRITS

RAGS

NEWSPAPERS

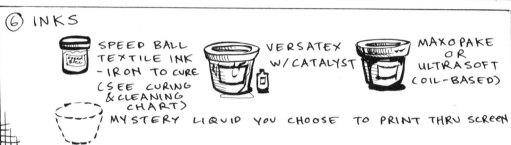

(6) INKS

SPEED BALL TEXTILE INK – IRON TO CURE (SEE CURING & CLEANING CHART)

VERSATEX W/ CATALYST

MAXOPAKE OR ULTRASOFT (OIL-BASED)

MYSTERY LIQUID YOU CHOOSE TO PRINT THRU SCREEN

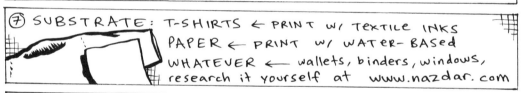

(7) SUBSTRATE: T-SHIRTS ← PRINT W/ TEXTILE INKS
PAPER ← PRINT W/ WATER-BASED
WHATEVER ← wallets, binders, windows, research it yourself at www.nazdar.com

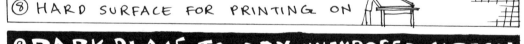

(8) HARD SURFACE FOR PRINTING ON

(9) **DARK PLACE TO DRY UNEXPOSED SCREEN**

(10) 75 WATT LIGHT BULBS (2)

OR

BBA NO. 1 PHOTOFLOOD 250 WATT

OR EXPOSURE UNIT

CLIP-ON DESK LAMP (TWO)

TO BE EXPLAINED IN ISSUE ③

(11) PIECE OF GLASS — TO HOLD DOWN TWO (2) !!
(12) TRANSPARENCIES
(13) BLACK PAPER TO GO UNDER SCREEN WHILE IT EXPOSES
(14) KNOWLEDGE!

CURING & CLEANING

"CURE: TO PREPARE OR ALTER ESPECIALLY BY CHEMICAL OR PHYSICAL PROCESSING FOR KEEPING OR USE" —webster's

CURING IS HOW THE INK IS DRIED SO THAT IT FORMS A PERMANENT BOND TO THE FABRIC AND WILL NOT WASH OUT.

INK*	USE	CURING	PROS	CONS	CLEAN-UP
Speedball Permanent Acrylic (water-based)	Paper or Fabric	Heat 275°-375° for 5 minutes**	Waterproof Breathable: fabric absorbs ink.	Brittle/cracks Fades a little Can't print light on dark	Water/hose
Maxopake Ultrasoft (oil-based)	Fabric	Heat using dryer (show below) 350°-5 min	Permanent Waterproof Stretchy Light on dark	Needs to be cured with a dryer* or flash-cure	Mineral spirits/rag
Versatex	Fabric	Chemical catalyst must be mixed into ink before printing	Permanent Waterproof Light on dark	Brittle/cracks dries extremely quickly in your screen (and will clog in permanently.)	Water- FAST!

** Use household iron

BORN HOMINS

FLASH OR SPOT DRYER

vent outside→

ON/OFF

Heating Elements

Track

*For more types of <u>ink</u> go to: www.nazdar.com

SCREENPRINTER PROFILE: MONICA CANILAO

What inspired you to start screen-printing?

I wanted to be able to make and put images where I wanted to and for free. I also had very inspiring art teachers in high school that went out of their way to make limited resources available.

What type of surfaces do you print on?

I make patches, print into mixed media art, on other types of prints, and clothing.

What types of ink do you use?

I use mainly water-based inks just because I don't have any sort of set up to mess with oil... too many chemicals. Most of the ink I like using best are weird brands I've never seen in stores, stuff I've picked up from the Creative Reuse Centers around the Bay Area. I have a bunch of reject textiles inks that I like the consistency of that are from the "Advanced color & chemical Corporation", Hunt Speedball textile printing ink- that's old and packaged like Oneshot, and a brand of professional inks I bought through a screen printing class I took a few years ago, and that crappy brand of speedball ink that you can find in any art store. When I want to print in neon I use liquid acrylic paint because it comes out very bright and it's easier to come by than the neon inks that actually work well. You just have to be careful and keep it damp because acrylic can really mess up your screen if you let it dry in the mesh.

What size print runs do you do?

Whatever I feel like. The last one was 500, but that wasn't up to me... it involved Yerba Buena and many people helping. Most times it's between 30 and 60. Sometimes it's just one.

How many colors do you generally use per design?

If it's a patch I generally use one or two colors. With paper I like to work with multiple layers of color and media, like spray paint, different papers and glue. I generally use around three or four colors with any one design. You can do a lot with layering... by printing on interesting paper, or thining down your inks and design your image so that layers overlap to create new

How do you separate and register colors?

I've never used Photoshop to make separations, but I hear it's easier. I usually draw or think out my image then transfer each layer onto vellum with film ink (Black India, Ultradraw Rapidograph 3085-F ink for paper & film works the absolute best, plus it's waterproof) and brush directly. You can use a razor blade to take out mistakes or scratch out details. For very flat color I'll use rubylith plus ink on vellum for lines and texture. If I want to reproduce an picture or drawing I already have I'll photocopy a black and white image of it onto photocopy acetate. In order to use those you need to make two exact duplicates of the image so that you can layer them. If you don't do this, the one copy will not be dark enough to burn into the screen correctly. When you use photocopies you also have to make sure you either cut out or scrape off any grey areas because those will show up when you burn your screen. Transparencies work especially well if you're using lots of text, detail, or thin lines.

How do you protect yourself from toxic materials such as inks and solvents while printing / cleaning up?

I don't.

Where do you print?

Most printing I do at home on my floor or bed. I always keep burned screens and materials around my house. For larger or more involved paper runs I'll sneak into the print shop at my old school in the night.

What are the benefits of screen printing?

You can reproduce almost any kind of image without too much equipment (like a press) or expertise. It's easy to learn how to do, keep screens around, and even travel with (like if you're a band on tour). If you save the transparencies for your images, you can always reburn them to print again. I think screen printing is the most versatile form of printmaking there is because you can use so many techniques to create the exact image you want, and print on almost anything so long as it's flat.

Where can we see your work?

I have a website that has a print section.
->>>---> Wewillallbewell.com or monicacanilao.com

What is the social, political, or environmental importance of screenprinting to you?

I don't think the prints I make necessarily focus on or create any sort of impact along those terms. I do however appreciate how others have used screen printing to spread their ideas and create beautiful things which effect other people.

What is the biggest screen printing disaster, success, or challenge you've ever had?

Trying to print a run of five hundred, 3 color posters in two days for Yerba Buena. Draw and separate the design the day before. The first day we lost a night of printing because the screens where not burning correctly- hours of stress with zero payoff. The next night different screens had to be defogged with those horrible chemicals just to make sure they would burn right before we could use them to print. That same night we ran through multiple colors at once with only a few people printing and pulling.

The funny part is, originally I was just supposed to be designing the image and mixing the colors for it. After I got there I ended up printing through the night and into morning. The task was so ridiculously large and hectic... it was fun in a sick, running your body into the ground, kind of way. Two of the girls helping where recovering from various bike wreck injuries- Amy's collar bone had been broken so she could only use one arm and one whole side of Sydney's body was swollen and covered with bruises, so she could only put weight on one of her legs while printing. I think we started with ten or so people helping. By the end there where three of us still running two colors until 5 or 6am.

DO-IT-YOURSELF SILKSCREENING #2

NOW THAT YOU PRINTED ONE HUNDRED T-SHIRTS, WHAT ARE YOU GONNA DO WITH THEM?

~ OR ~

"HOW TO MAKE A MILLION DOLLARS SELLING T-SHIRTS ON THE STREET"

TRIAL & TRIBULATION ON TELEGRAPH AVENUE

A year ago, I finished a comic called "Do-It-Yourself Silkscreening" which explained the process of printing t-shirts at home.

This second issue is less "How-To" and more autobiographical. While most of the events described here really happend, the characters (other than myself) are all fictional. If any of my fellow street vendors feels offended or disturbed by my depictions of street vendors, I offer my apologies in advance. Please know that I meant no ill will against you, I only wished to depict a day in the life of a street vendor.

I had a great time selling t-shirts on Telegraph, and I did sell a great many more t-shirts than you see me selling in this comic. I would like to thank all the vendors for sharing their advice, stories, good humor and good cheer with me.

John Isaacson 2005

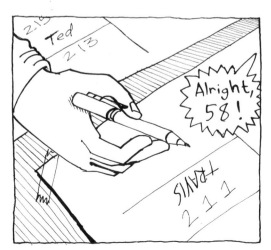

41

43

44

45

47

49

You have your cowboys...

...hippies and poets...

...punk rock teenagers...

...pretending they aren't here with their parents...

...rappers and jocks...

...professors and students...

52

57

Hey man- You did these shirts?

Yeah

Me and my crew are gonna do shirts too- They're gonna be HUGE

Hey- where do you get them printed at?

In my living room

Oh

Cool

well

I'll be back later

Alright

Hey! Battlebeasts! Transformers! Robotech! I remember those!

Maybe I'll be back later

Too bad I ain't got any money

ECONO CHRIST

ANOTHER VICTIM

Hey dude, getting a lot of "I.B.B.L."s?

What's an "I.B.B.L"?

"I'll Be Back Later"

But they never come back

They NEVER come back!

It's probably like a game to them - they're probably seeing how many I.B.B.Ls they can get in one day!

Yeah! Like: "I got FIVE I.B.B.Ls today! How many did you get?"

They're probably just goin' up and down the street sayin' "I'll be back later! I'll be back later! I'll be back later!" to all the vendors!

Ha ha!

Naw - it's cool... People are just shopping...

Yeah...

How do all these vendors SURVIVE out here? There's hardly any money to be made!

Most of these vendors must be on the verge of homelessness!

Hey. You see that vendor over there?

Hm? Who?

That old guy selling tie-dyed shirts

Oh, yeah.

That's RANDY

He's been out here since 1968

Wow

he's my uncle

Back then you didn't have to buy a license to vend

You didn't have to pay $140???

Nope

The city didn't regulate it. There was no lottery system.

Vendors had to claim their own spots then

They would pay the homeless to guard their spots at night

And then — at like, three in the morning, they would **brawl** to get more space!

Even if it was just for five more inches!

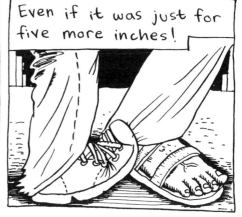

In the morning the vendors would come back and ask:

How much space didja' get?

'bout five inches

And they would tip 'em a few extra bucks if they got some more space!

Thanks man!

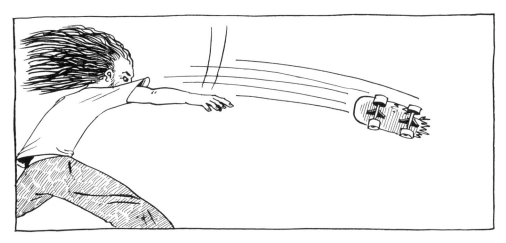

65

Hey Isaac?

Huh?

Nina wants to know if she can draw with you

We got her an art set with all these pens... but we forgot to bring any paper...

Prismacolors! Alright! Ya wanna come draw Nina?

I'll get her chair

Whadda ya wanna draw?

SCREENPRINTER PROFILE: HOT IRON PRESS

What inspired you to start screen-printing?

Kyle first learned to screenprint from our friend Anna, who was printing her own Action Patrol patches. Jenny taught herself how to silkscreen with the somewhat helpful but often misleading manual that comes inside of one of those cheap Speedball screenprinting kits. We both instantly realized the great potential silkscreening held for easily reproducing all kinds of cool stuff – not only patches, but also t-shirts, stickers, posters, etc. Later on, after studying printmaking in school for a few years, we came to love silkscreening as opposed to other printmaking processes for its speed, efficiency, and relatively low expense.

What type of surfaces do you print on?

Anything and everything on paper – posters, record covers, business cards, wedding invitations, etc. Though, we can also print on unusual surfaces if the need arises.

What types of ink do you use?

99% of the time we stick with water based ink. It's less toxic and so much easier to clean up than solvent or other kinds of inks. We mix our own inks by using about 1/2 acrylic paint, 1/2 transparent base, and then a tiny amount of some type of retarder (like glycerine, aqualube, or acrylic retarding medium) to keep it from drying in the screen.

What size print runs do you do? (100's - 10's?)

It depends on the project. We typically print in the 100's. The biggest job we've ever done was 1000 4-color cd covers. But of course, we occasionally do very small runs too (100 or less).

How many colors do you generally use per design?

We try to keep the number of colors to a minimum when working with clients because it keeps the cost down for them. We like to try to print on a colored paper so that we can use the color of the paper as a color in the image, but when we're working on our own stuff we print as many colors as is necessary.

How do you separate and register colors? (on a computer - photoshop - illustrator / by hand with sharpie and vellum / with stencils).

Typically we use Photoshop to do any design work or separations. We print out our positives onto paper on a copy shop's oversize printer (and make our photocopy translucent for burning by rubbing a thin layer of veggie oil onto both sides of it). For registration during printing, we just make sure that the screen is very securely held in a pair of hinged clamps, and then mark off the proper placement of two sides and a corner with masking tape. We usually triple-up or quadruple-up the masking tape until it is as thick as the substrate we are printing on so that it's very easy to quickly pop each print into place. We sometimes use mylar if the registration has to be perfect, and the edition size is small, but the tape method has proven itself most useful for us the bulk of the time. A vacuum table helps a lot with registration as it keeps the paper on the mark while you move the screen. We built our own with pegboard, shopvac, and a rubber liner from the hardware store.

How do you protect yourself from toxic materials such as inks and solvents while printing / cleaning up?

Our inks are non-toxic, so that's not a concern. The most toxic thing we use is the photo emulsion which is "known to the State of California" to be cancer-causing. We just do our best to keep it from touching our skin, or wear gloves when working with it.

Where do you print?

We live and work in the same building. We have an apartment on the second floor, and directly below that lies our shop where we do all our silkscreening and letterpress work.

What do you listen to while you print?

We like to listen to all kinds of music while we work, though it can be hard to hear it sometimes over the sound of the vacuum table.

Where can we see your work?

www.hotironpress.com

22/28

SCREENPRINTER PROFILE: DARIA TESSLER

What inspired you to start screen-printing?

liking a process that allows for total independence while letting me make multiples. i get too clingy when i make things that are one of a kind. this way i can give things to friends and have work to sell affordably to folks.

What type of surfaces do you print on? (Paper - comic covers - posters - fine art / Fabric - Clothing - patches / Other materials - glass - wood...)

all of the above plus formica counter tops

What types of ink do you use?

nazdar is the jam. nazdar for paper, water based, plus random stuff, often with a little scooplet of union aerotex textile waterbased ink to keep the nazdar from getting too thick and sticky plus a few drops of speedball retarder. that stuff saves my life every time.

What size print runs do you do? (100's - 10's?)

usually around 30, but for book covers around 100

How many colors do you generally use per design?

3-7

How do you separate and register colors?

by hand, use registration tabs and acetate on shirts or when my tabs fail me

How do you protect yourself from toxic materials such as inks and solvents while printing / cleaning up?

the only really toxic thing is the stencil remover and i use latex gloves because it makes my hands fall to pieces if i don't. i get to hang out in the backyard with a hose wearing latex gloves like a creep . my housemates think its very funny.

Where do you print?

in my new double bedroom!

What do you listen to while you print?

i used to be superstitious about stevie wonder making my printing go well, but once i'd over done it with the 60's/70's stuff and embraced his 80's work i knew it was time to move on. rap is good. italian disco is good.

Where can we see your work?

www.animalsleepstories.com, otsu and sometimes giant robot sf

DO-IT-TOGETHER SCREENPRINTING #3

BY JOHN ISAACSON

DREAM JOB OR NIGHTMARE JOB?

Sometimes it's hard to tell. Call it a "career change", having a "Saturn return", or "following your dreams", but many people reach a point where they want to turn their weekend hobby into a full-time job. You can only get so far "Doing It Yourself" before you need some advice or help from your peers, co-workers, collaborators, and mentors.

In this third chapter of Do-It-Yourself Silkscreen we see the amateur hobbyist enter the realm of professional-level technology. Isaac tries to take his craft up to the next level of multiple-color prints and mass-production, but lacks the knowledge and experience to do so. He learns from Candace, a seasoned pre-press technician, and Nate, a somewhat jaded printer, that the materials involved with mass production are highly expensive, hazardous to one's health, and not exactly DIY.

Screenprinting is an eighty-billion-dollar-a-year industry. Manufacturers produce inks, squeegees, emulsion and screens for printing not only on fabric and paper, but also wood, glass, plastic, metal, and vinyl. Everything from beer bottles to bumper stickers, and circuit boards to ceramic mugs are screen-printed.

However, screenprinting is also an effective way to produce and distribute your own media with little overhead cost or environmental impact if you print on recycled materials. While the level of technical detail in this chapter may be too much for some, things like mesh count, off-contact, and screen tension all effect the quality of prints. whether you're printing in the professional field, in class, or at home.

FIVE MINUTES ROLL BY...

HI! I'M CANDACE

THE OWNER'S NOT HERE BUT I CAN SHOW YOU AROUND THE SHOP A LITTLE BIT

I'M ISAAC

YOU'LL BE TAKING CUSTOMER'S ARTWORK TO THE COMPUTER AND PRINTING OUT COLOR SEPARATIONS

OR YOU CAN SCAN THEIR ARTWORK ON THIS SCANNER — IT HAS TO BE AT LEAST A HUNDRED AND FIFTY D.P.I.

WHAT'S D.P.I.?

DOTS PER INCH

THAT'S RESO-LUTION

SEVENTY-TWO DOTS-PER-INCH IS WHAT YOU SEE ON A COMPUTER SCREEN

BUT THAT'S TOO LOW FOR PRINTING OUT A HARD COPY — IT LOOKS ALL JAGGED AND PIXELATED

SEE?

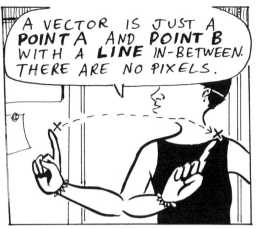

THE INTERVIEW

THE NEXT DAY...

HI ISAAC, I'M DAVE NICE TA MEETCHA

HI DAVE I'M ISAAC

SO CANDACE TELLS ME YA KNOW HOW TO BURN SCREENS BUT YER NOT SO HOT ON THE COMPUTER STUFF

BUT I DO KNOW PHOTOSHOP

CANDACE - WHAT'S THAT ONE WE USE?

ILLUSTRATOR

WELL HOW DIFFERENT ARE THEY?

NOT REALLY

CANDACE, ARE THEY DIFFERENT?

THEY'RE DIFFERENT

SEE, I DON'T KNOW CRAP ABOUT COMPUTERS

"WHEN I STARTED OUT IN THIS BUSINESS WE PHOTO-GRAPHED ART WORK AND CUT OUT STENCILS TO SEPARATE COLORS"

TRIPPY HIPPY JAM BAND

SO CANDACE IS GONNA SHOW YOU HOW TO USE ILLUSTRATOR- SEE IF YOU CAN GET THE HANG OF IT. I'M GONNA GO BLOW-OUT SOME SHIRTS

87

COLOR SEPARATIONS

THIS IS THE CUSTOMER'S ARTWORK. WE'VE ADDED REGISTRATION MARKS AT THE TOP AND BOTTOM OF THE IMAGE

ONE LOVE
VIBRATION

WE HORIZONTALLY ALIGN AND CENTER THE REG. MARKS

WINDOWS > ALIGN
⇧ F7

THEN GROUP EVERYTHING

OBJECT > ALIGN
⌘ G

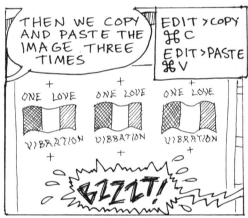

THEN WE COPY AND PASTE THE IMAGE THREE TIMES

EDIT > COPY
⌘ C
EDIT > PASTE
⌘ V

BZZZT!

THEN WE LOCK THREE OF THEM SO WE DON'T ACCIDENTALLY SELECT THEM

OBJECT > LOCK
⌘ 2

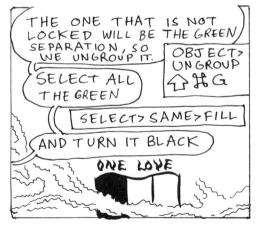

THE ONE THAT IS NOT LOCKED WILL BE THE GREEN SEPARATION, SO WE UNGROUP IT.

OBJECT > UNGROUP
⇧ ⌘ G

SELECT ALL THE GREEN

SELECT > SAME > FILL

AND TURN IT BLACK

ONE LOVE

THEN SELECT ALL THE OTHER COLORS THAT AREN'T GREEN AND TURN THEM WHITE.

ONE + GREEN

BZZZT

TYPE "GREEN" NEXT TO THE REGISTRATION MARKS AND YOU'RE DONE WITH THE GREEN.

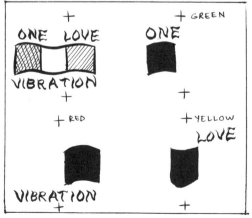

BEFORE WE TAPE UP THESE FILMS I'M GONNA SHOW YOU HOW TO COAT SCREENS, AND WHERE WE KEEP THE DIFFERENT MESHES

WHY IS THE LIGHT RED IN HERE?

THAT LIGHT BULB IS RED SO THE SCREENS DON'T EXPOSE

SEE? THE EMULSION ON THESE SCREENS IS THE EXACT SAME LIGHT-RED COLOR AS THE LIGHT CAST BY THE BULB.

OH! SO THE ONLY LIGHT IN HERE IS BEING **REFLECTED BY** THE EMULSION

AND NOT **ABSORBED**

THESE SCREENS IN THE DRYING RACK ARE DRY NOW. YOU CAN STACK THEM ON THE FLOOR

RIGHT HERE?

WE USE THE 82'S TO PRINT WHITE INK ON BLACK SHIRTS - THEY HAVE THE WIDEST MESH AND THAT INK IS REALLY THICK

THE 110'S ARE A GOOD GENERIC MESH - YOU CAN PRINT PRETTY MUCH ANYTHING THROUGH THEM

THE 156'S ARE FOR PRINTING DARK INKS ON LIGHT SHIRTS - IF THEY HAVE A LOT OF DETAIL

WE ONLY USE THE 305'S FOR PRINTING REALLY FINE HALF-TONE DOTS OR FOR PRINTING WITH PROCESS INKS

WHAT ARE PROCESS INKS?

FOUR-COLOR PROCESS: CYAN, MAGENTA, YELLOW, BLACK OR "CMYK". IT'S HOW NEWSPAPERS ARE PRINTED

BY COMBINING DIFFERENT SIZE DOTS OF THOSE FOUR COLORS YOU CAN CREATE ALMOST ANY OTHER COLOR

BUT I DON'T REALLY THINK THE TECHNOLOGY TRANSFERS THAT WELL TO FABRIC

THAT'S WHY I'M A SCREEN-PRINTER, I GUESS: I LIKE BIG, FLAT, SOLID COLORS, NO BULLSHIT GRADIENTS

SO HAVE YOU EVER USED ONE OF THESE BEFORE?

WHAT IS IT?

IT'S AN EMULSION-COATER! HOW DO YOU COAT YOUR SCREENS AT HOME?

CARDBOARD

YOU USE CARDBOARD??? OH MY GOD — THAT'S TOO FUNNY! HA HA

SO WE JUST POUR THE EMULSION INTO THE COATER

HAND ME AN UN-COATED SCREEN

THANKS

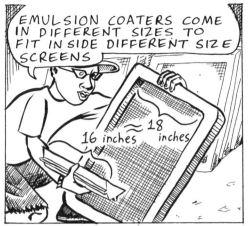

EMULSION COATERS COME IN DIFFERENT SIZES TO FIT INSIDE DIFFERENT SIZE SCREENS

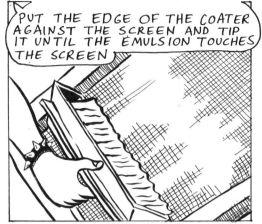

PUT THE EDGE OF THE COATER AGAINST THE SCREEN AND TIP IT UNTIL THE EMULSION TOUCHES THE SCREEN

WHEN YOU START COATING, LEAN THE SCREEN BACK

THEN TILT IT TOWARDS THE OPPOSITE SIDE AS YOU PULL THE COATER UP

THAT WAY, WHEN YOU PULL THE COATER AWAY FROM THE SCREEN, NO DRIPS FALL ON THE SCREEN

THEN YOU DO THE SAME THING ON THE BACK-SIDE OF THE SCREEN

AGAIN, ROTATE THE SCREEN AS YOU PULL THE COATER UP SO NO DRIPS FALL ON THE SCREEN

IF ANY DRIPS FALL ON THE SCREEN, THE EMULSION WILL BE TOO THICK TO WASH OUT AFTER YOU'VE EXPOSED THE SCREEN.

CONVERSELY, IF THE EMULSION IS TOO THIN, THEN TINY SPOTS OF THE SCREEN WON'T GET COATED

WE CALL THEM "PINHOLES". YOU CAN SEE LIGHT SHINING THROUGH THEM

ALSO, IF YOUR SCREEN COATER HAS ANY CHIPS, DINGS, OR SCRATCHES IN IT, THOSE CAN CAUSE STREAKS IN YOUR EMULSION

DRIPS, PINHOLES, AND STREAKS ARE ALL REASONS TO RE-COAT THE SCREEN IN ORDER TO GET AN EVEN COAT OF EMULSION

THIS SCREEN IS EIGHTEEN INCHES WIDE

SO NINE INCHES WILL MEASURE IN TO THE CENTER OF THE SCREEN, RIGHT?

THEREFORE, WE PLACE THE REGISTRATION MARKS EXACTLY NINE INCHES IN FROM THE EDGE OF THE SCREEN, HORIZONTALLY

WE MEASURE TO THE CENTER OF THE SCREEN BECAUSE THIS IMAGE GOES ON THE CENTER OF THE SHIRT

IT'S ALWAYS SAFE TO MEASURE TWO INCHES DOWN, FROM THE EDGE OF THE EMULSION

EXPOSURE

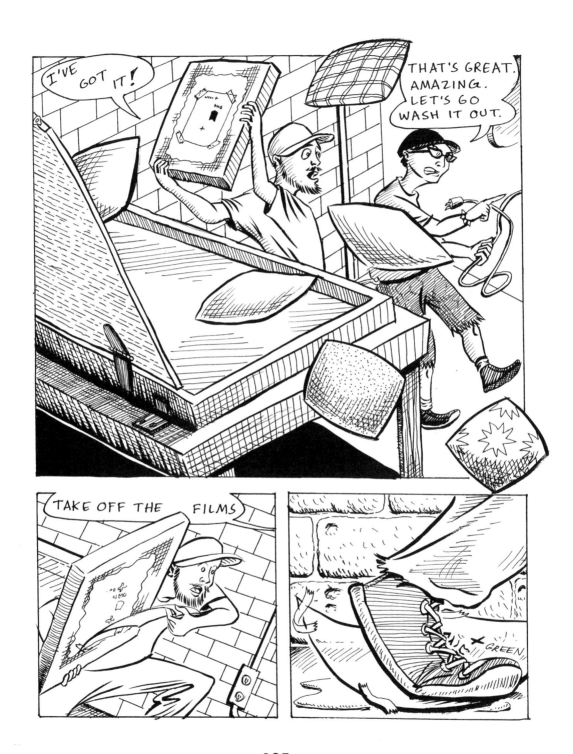

105

WASHOUT

EACH KNOB ALLOWS THE SCREEN TO BE REPOSITIONED AND SECURED

CLAMP TIGHTENERS

CLAMP

WHEN LOOSENED THESE KNOBS ALLOW THE SCREEN TO ROTATE TO THE RIGHT AND LEFT

SCREEN GOES IN HERE

OFF-CONTACT ADJUSTMENT

HORIZONTAL ADJUSTMENT

CLAMPS ARE IN RAISED POSITION

CLAMPS CAN BE EITHER RAISED OR LOWERED

ENTIRE CAROUSEL UNIT ROTATES 360° TO THE RIGHT AND LEFT

YOU CAN LOOSEN THE PALLETS

AND SLIDE THEM BACK AND FORTH UNDER THE SCREEN

IT'S GOOD FOR SUPPORT IF THE SCREEN FRAME COMES INTO CONTACT WITH THE PALLET

BECAUSE IF ONLY THE SCREEN MESH HITS THE PALLET IT MIGHT RIP OR TEAR?

EXACTLY

CENTERING THE SCREEN

WE'LL DRAW A LINE DOWN THE CENTER OF THE PALLET

12 inches

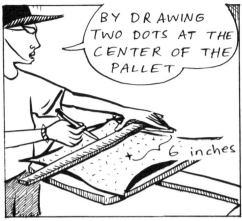

BY DRAWING TWO DOTS AT THE CENTER OF THE PALLET

6 inches

AND CONNECTING THOSE DOTS

NOW WE'VE GOT OUR CENTERING LINE...

WE CAN CENTER THE SCREEN

WHILE THERE'S NO INK ON THE SCREEN, YOU CAN KINDA SEE THROUGH THE EMULSION SEE HOW IT'S NOT CENTERED?

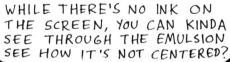

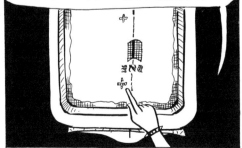

OFF-CONTACT

WE CAN USE THE HORIZONTAL ADJUSTMENT TO BRING THE SCREEN OVER SLIGHTLY

SEE HOW BOTH REGISTRATION MARKS LINE UP ON THE CENTERING LINE WE DREW?

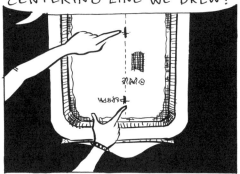

NOW THAT THE SCREEN IS CENTERED, WE ALSO NEED TO MAKE SURE THERE IS A LITTLE DISTANCE BETWEEN THE BOTTOM OF THE SCREEN AND THE PALLET—THIS DISTANCE IS CALLED THE **OFF-CONTACT** DISTANCE *

YOU WANT THE INK TO ONLY TOUCH THE SHIRT WHEN YOU'RE PUTTING PRESSURE DOWN WITH THE SQUEEGEE

CONTACT

TAPE-OUT

YOU CAN ADJUST THE OFF-CONTACT DISTANCE BY LOOSENING THIS KNOB

NOW WE NEED TO TAPE OUT THESE OPEN AREAS WHERE INK CAN STILL PASS THROUGH THE SCREEN

I USE THIS BLUE REMOVABLE PAINTER'S TAPE ON THE SCREEN

SKRITCH!

HOW COME?

BECAUSE IT LEAVES NO GUMMY RESIDUE ON THE SCREEN

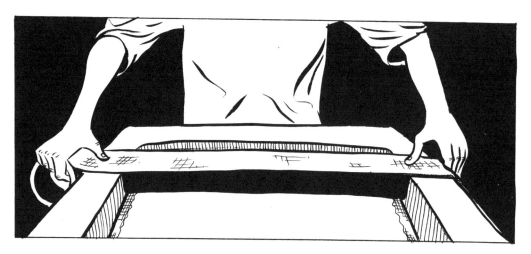

RIP!

THAT'S A LOT OF TAPE YOU'RE USING!

YEAH- WE GO THROUGH A LOT OF TAPE HERE- BUT WE HAVE TO IN ORDER TO KEEP INK FROM GOING THROUGH THE GUTTERS!

INK

CAN YOU GRAB ME A CUP OF THE GREEN INK OVER THERE?

DON'T THE INKS DRY OUT SITTING HERE?

NO—THEY NEVER DRY OUT, BECAUSE THESE ARE OIL-BASED, OR SOLVENT-BASED INKS

OH

BUT THEY DO GET STIFF WHEN THEY SIT FOR TOO LONG—CAN YOU GIVE IT A STIR?

ALL THOSE SCREENS HAVE BEEN SITTING THERE FOR MONTHS WITH INK ON THEM--IT'S STILL WET

OH—THAT'S THE KELLEY GREEN—IT'S TOO LIGHT

WHAT ABOUT THIS FOREST GREEN?

WE'LL HAVE TO MIX THEM TOGETHER

TOO DARK!

OH YEAH

THE ONLY SAMPLE WE HAVE FOR COLOR-MATCHING IS THEIR DIGITAL FILE-WHICH IS RGB COLOR, SO WE CAN'T MATCH IT EXACTLY!

RGB STANDS FOR RED, GREEN, BLUE-IT'S COLOR THAT IS PROJECTED BY LIGHT SHINING THROUGH IT FROM A TV OR COMPUTER MONITOR

ALL OTHER COLORS (LIKE THIS INK) ARE REFLECTING DAYLIGHT OR OVERHEAD LIGHT INTO OUR EYES

UNFORTUNATELY THIS CLIENT DIDN'T GIVE US ANY PANTONE NUMBERS, SO WE'RE GONNA HAVE TO EYEBALL IT.

THIS IS A MEDIUM GREEN SO WE'LL USE THREE-QUARTERS KELLY AND ONE QUARTER FOREST

HERE'S A NEW CUP

THANKS

WHY DON'T YOU STIR IT UP?

JUST TRY NOT TO GET ANY IN YOUR BEARD!

HA!

UGH! THESE INKS STINK!

IS IT CLOSE?

YES

LET'S GET THIS PARTY STARTED!

SQUEEGEES

SQUEEGEES COME IN DIFFERENT HARDNESSES- CALLED DUROMETER

SOFT ONES PUSH MORE INK

HARD ONES PUSH LESS INK

60'S

90'S

A SQUEEGEE WITH A DUROMETER OF 70-75 IS WHAT YOU WANT TO USE *

DUROMETERS OF 60 OR LESS ARE USED FOR A THICK INK DEPOSIT

SOFT SQUEEGEE

PUFF PAINT OR WHITE INK

82 MESH SCREEN

THICK INK DEPOSIT

DUROMETERS OF 70 ARE AVERAGE FOR PRINTING ON FABRIC

MEDIUM SQUEEGEE

110-156 MESH SCREEN

MEDIUM INK DEPOSIT

DUROMETERS OF 80 AND ABOVE ARE GENERALLY USED TO PRINT ON PAPER

HARD SQUEEGEE

195 MESH SCREEN

THIN INK DEPOSIT

YOU ALSO SHOULD SELECT A SQUEEGEE THAT IS THE CORRECT WIDTH FOR YOUR PRINT

YOU SHOULD HOLD THE SQUEEGEE AT A 65-80° ANGLE ǂ

OH, I THOUGHT IT WAS 45°

NO

* SOURCE: "CHOOSING THE RIGHT SQUEEGEE" BY TERRY COMBS
ǂ SOURCE: SCREENPRINTING TODAY BY ANDY McDOUGAL

PRINTING

THIS IS THE FLOOD STROKE: I'M ONLY COVERING THE STENCIL WITH INK SO IT IS PRIMED TO PRINT, HOWEVER, I'M **NOT** PUTTING DOWN ANY PRESSURE, SO THE OFF-CONTACT DISTANCE IS MAINTAINED

FLOOD

NOW THAT THE SCREEN IS FLOODED, I CAN PRINT BY PUTTING DOWN EVEN PRESSURE WITH A HAND ON EACH SIDE OF THE SQUEEGEE SO THE SCREEN IS PRESSED DOWN INTO CONTACT WITH THE PALLET

PRINT

YOU ALWAYS PRINT IN THE SAME DIRECTION; TOP TO BOTTOM - YOU CAN DRAG THE SQUEEGEE THE OPPOSITE DIRECTION WHEN YOU FLOOD, BUT NEVER PUSH THE SQUEE-GEE DOWN IN THE OPPOSITE DIRECTION

RE-FLOOD

COLOR REGISTRATION

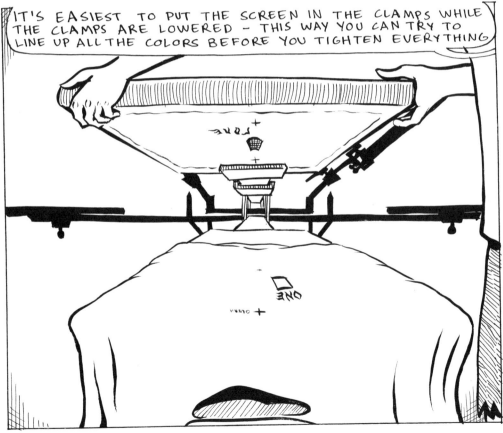

BECAUSE WE CENTERED THE FILMS ON THE SCREENS BEFORE EXPOSING THE IMAGE...

...WE SHOULD BE ABLE TO ALIGN THE COLORS WITHOUT TOO MUCH TROUBLE

ONCE YOU'VE EYEBALLED THE REGISTRATION, YOU CAN TIGHTEN THE CLAMPS STARTING WITH THOSE CLOSEST TO THE SCREEN, AND THEN MOVING BACKWARDS, AWAY FROM THE SCREEN

① SCREEN CLAMPS

② SCREEN-BACK ADJUSTMENT

③ OFF-CONTACT ADJUSTMENT

④ MAIN REGISTRATION CLAMPS

⑤ HORIZONTAL ADJUSTMENT

BECAUSE OF THE OFF-CONTACT DISTANCE BETWEEN THE SCREEN AND THE PRINT...

...LOOKING THROUGH THE SCREEN ONLY GIVES YOU A GENERAL, RATHER THAN A SPECIFIC IDEA OF WHERE THE PRINT WILL LAND

SOMETIMES IT HELPS TO PUSH DOWN ON THE SCREEN TOO SEE WHERE THE PRINT WILL LAND.

SOME OF THE GREEN INK THAT WAS STILL WET WAS TRANSFERRED FROM THE SHIRT TO THE BACK OF THE YELLOW SCREEN WHEN WE PUSHED THE SCREEN DOWN TO LOOK THROUGH IT

ACTUALLY, IT'S IN TWO PLACES ON THE BACK OF THE YELLOW SCREEN—ONCE WHERE IT IS ALIGNED, AND ONCE WHERE IT ISN'T

THE GREEN INK THAT IS NOT LINED UP WILL COME OFF AFTER A FEW PRINTS, BUT WE CAN ALSO DO THIS:

USE TAPE?

YEAH. SEE HOW EASILY IT COMES OFF?

BUT IT'S STILL ON OVER HERE— IT WILL ALWAYS BE GETTING PICKED UP OVER THERE—

AS LONG AS THIS IS A WET-ON-WET PRINT

EVEN THE RED SCREEN MAY PICK UP A LITTLE OF THE GREEN INK

PUSHING DOWN ON THE SCREEN MAY GIVE YOU A CLOSER IDEA OF WHERE THE PRINT WILL LAND, BUT DON'T PUSH TOO MUCH!

SCREEN TENSION

BECAUSE THE SCREEN MIGHT RIP?

OR JUST GET LOOSE - SCREENS NEED TO STAY TIGHT IN ORDER TO REGISTER CONSISTENTLY

SCREEN MANUFACTURERS STRETCH SCREENS TO A TENSION OF 30-40 NEWTONS PER CENTIMETER

WHAT'S THAT?

THIS IS A SCREEN TENSION METER ✱

SEE? THIS SCREEN IS GETTING A LITTLE OLD - WE SHOULD HAVE IT RE-STRETCHED

DOES THAT MEAN YOU LOSE THE STENCIL?

YES, IT WOULD HAVE NEW MESH ON THE OLD FRAME

BUT CAN WE STILL USE THIS ONE?

20-30 NEWTONS IS ACCEPTABLE - IT SHOULDN'T GET ANY LOWER THAN 2-3 NEWTONS

I GUESS I CAN RE-STRETCH MY OWN SCREENS AT HOME WITHOUT LOSING THE STENCIL BECAUSE MINE ARE ONLY STAPLED TO THE FRAME!

YEAH - TRY NOT TO GET TANGLED UD IN THE TAPE THIS TIME

✱ Veeeery expensive!

YOU DON'T NEED TO PUSH TOO HARD TO GET THE RED TO SHOW UP BECAUSE IT'S SUCH A DARK, SATURATED COLOR. YOU ONLY NEED TO PULL IT ONCE

ONCE?

EACH TIME YOU PRINT WITH THE SQUEEGEE, YOU'RE PUTTING DOWN ANOTHER LAYER OF INK —WE CALL THESE "PULLS"

WE SHOULD DO TWO PULLS OF THE YELLOW— IT'S TOO LIGHT

UH-OH: THE RED NEEDS TO BE ROTATED CLOCK-WISE

THERE'S ALSO A RED DOT COMING THROUGH

LET'S FIND ANOTHER SPOT TO PRINT ON THIS SHIRT, RE-PRINT THE GREEN AND YELLOW, THEN WE'LL RE-ADJUST THE RED

d'oh!

AFTER RE-PRINTING THE GREEN AND YELLOW...

SO WE LOOSEN THESE?

NO! LEAVE THOSE ALONE

WHEN YOU WANT TO ROTATE A SCREEN, YOU USE THE MICRO-REGISTRATION-TOOL

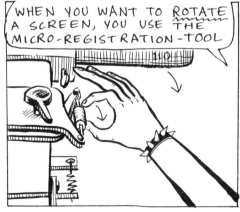

135

CHECKING THE CURE

WHAT IF ONE OF THOSE AEROSOL CANS FALLS IN?

WHAT, ARE YOU GOING TO TRY TO BLOW US ALL UP, MR. UNABOMBER?

WHEN A SHIRT COMES OUT OF THE DRYER THERE ARE TWO WAYS TO CHECK THE CURE

FIRST, YOU CAN SEE IF ANY INK COMES OFF ON YOUR FINGERS—

SECOND, YOU STRETCH THE FABRIC - THE OIL-BASED INK SHOULD STRETCH WITH THE FABRIC—

IF ANY HOLES APPEAR IN THE INK WHEN IT STRETCHES

137

WET-ON-WET

SO... WHAT ARE YOU DRINK-ER-PRINTING HERE?

RASTAMAN VIBRATIONS, DUDE!

=BURP!=

I SHOULD GET IRIE WHILE I PRINT THIS ONE!

UH- I DUNNO 'BOUT THAT

DUDE! I'M JUST KIDDING!

THIS IS A TOTALLY EASY PRINT! IT'LL GO BY FAST BECAUSE IT'S WET-ON-WET

WHAT'S WET-ON-WET?

"WHAT'S WET-ON-WET?" "??" DUDE, HOW DID YOU EVEN GET THIS JOB?. ARE YOU ALREADY HIRED?

UH- YEAH- I THINK SO

NONE OF THESE COLORS TOUCH OR OVERLAP- THEREFORE, WE CAN PRINT EACH COLOR SUCCESSIVELY WITHOUT HAVING TO DRY ANY OF THEM IN-BETWEEN

ONE LOVE

RATION

HOW WOULD YOU DRY THE PRINT BETWEEN COLORS WITHOUT MOVING THE SHIRT?

BY USING THE FLASH-DRYER

140

THE FLASH-DRYER

IF THIS WERE A PRINT THAT HAD ANY OVERLAPPING COLORS WE WOULD TURN ON THE FLASH DRYER, PARK IT OVER A PALLET AND IT WOULD DRY THE SHIRTS AS I ROTATE THEM UNDER IT

BUT YOU CAN ONLY LEAVE THE SHIRTS UNDER FOR 15-20 SECONDS OR ELSE THEY'LL BURN

YOW!

NAH, IT'S NOT SO BAD, SEE I CAN SHOW YA HOW IT WORKS —IT TAKES A WHILE TO HEAT UP

IT DOES THE SAME THING AS THE DRYER?

CLICK

VVMMM

YUP, ONLY WITHOUT TAKING THE SHIRT OFF THE PALLET, SO WHEN THE INK IS DRY, YOU CAN PRINT OVER IT WITH ANOTHER COLOR

WHY WOULD YOU DO THAT?

IF WE'RE PRINTING WHITE ON BLACK

OR ANY OTHER LIGHT COLOR ON A DARK FABRIC – IT'S HARD TO GET A COLOR TO PRINT EVENLY, SOLIDLY, AND OPAQUELY ON A BLACK SHIRT

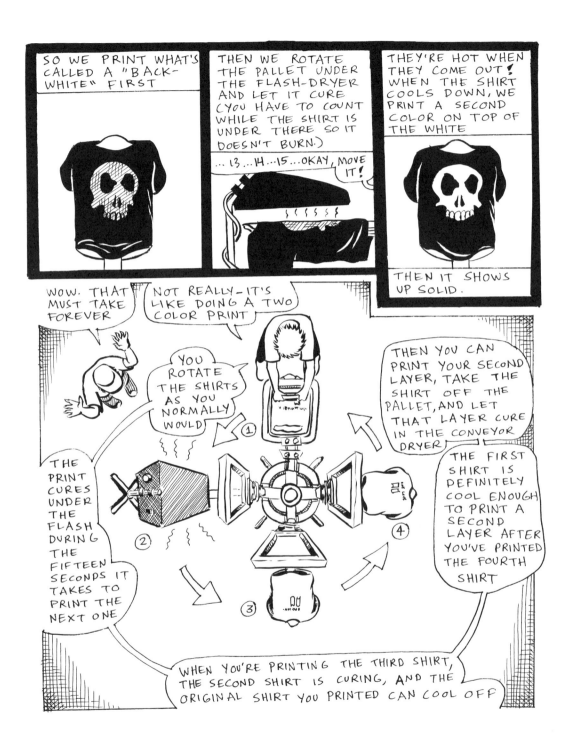

SO WE PRINT WHAT'S CALLED A "BACK-WHITE" FIRST

THEN WE ROTATE THE PALLET UNDER THE FLASH-DRYER AND LET IT CURE (YOU HAVE TO COUNT WHILE THE SHIRT IS UNDER THERE SO IT DOESN'T BURN.)

...13...14...15...OKAY, MOVE IT!

THEY'RE HOT WHEN THEY COME OUT! WHEN THE SHIRT COOLS DOWN, WE PRINT A SECOND COLOR ON TOP OF THE WHITE

THEN IT SHOWS UP SOLID.

WOW. THAT MUST TAKE FOREVER

NOT REALLY — IT'S LIKE DOING A TWO COLOR PRINT

YOU ROTATE THE SHIRTS AS YOU NORMALLY WOULD

THEN YOU CAN PRINT YOUR SECOND LAYER, TAKE THE SHIRT OFF THE PALLET, AND LET THAT LAYER CURE IN THE CONVEYOR DRYER

THE PRINT CURES UNDER THE FLASH DURING THE FIFTEEN SECONDS IT TAKES TO PRINT THE NEXT ONE

THE FIRST SHIRT IS DEFINITELY COOL ENOUGH TO PRINT A SECOND LAYER AFTER YOU'VE PRINTED THE FOURTH SHIRT

WHEN YOU'RE PRINTING THE THIRD SHIRT, THE SECOND SHIRT IS CURING, AND THE ORIGINAL SHIRT YOU PRINTED CAN COOL OFF

IF THE SHIRTS DON'T COOL DOWN BEFORE YOU PRINT THE SECOND LAYER, THE HEAT MAKES THE INK ALL RUNNY AND YOU GET A BLURRY PRINT!

SO IT HAS TO COOL DOWN COMPLETELY

YEAH

ONE LOVE VIBRATION

SO HOW COME YOU WANTED TO WORK HERE?

I PRINT MY OWN SHIRTS AND SELL THEM ON TELEGRAPH

SO, SAME REASON AS EVERY-ONE ELSE

WHAT'S THAT?

DUDE WE ALL WORK HERE 'CAUSE WE WANNA PRINT OUR OWN STUFF!

WHERE DO YOU KEEP IT?

OH—I JUST PRINT ON WHAT-EVER I'M WEARING AT THE TIME

ALL CUSTOMIZED, ONE-OF-A-KIND?

YEAH

THAT'S COOL...

RING

THANKS FOR CALLING PRO-SHIRTS, THIS IS ISAAC

ISAAC, IT'S CANDACE! CAN YOU CHECK E-MAIL, PRINT OUT SOME FILES I JUST SENT, AND BURN SCREENS FOR ME BEFORE DAVE GETS BACK?

144

RECLAIMING SCREENS

USE THESE PLASTIC SCRAPERS TO TAKE LEFTOVER INK OFF THE SCREEN AND SQUEEGEE

YOU CAN SAVE THE LEFT-OVER INK AND RE-USE IT

WE USE SOAP TO CLEAN OFF THE INK, RECLAIMER FOR REMOVING THE EMULSION, AND DEGREASER FOR RE-MOVING ANY RESIDUE OILS

WE HAVE TO KEEP THE SPONGES WE USE WITH EACH CHEMICAL SEPARATED FROM EACH OTHER

OKAY...

...BECAUSE IF YOU ACCIDENTALLY USE THE RECLAIMING SPONGE WHEN YOU'RE ONLY TRYING TO CLEAN OFF THE INK, THEN YOU'LL ACTUALLY REMOVE THE STENCIL!

USING GLOVES, WE SPRAY THE SCREENS WITH SOAP TO BREAK DOWN THE INK AND SCRUB THEM WITH A HEAVY-DUTY SPONGE

148

WHEN THE RECLAIMED SCREENS ARE DRY, THIS DEGREASER WILL NEUTRALIZE ALL RESIDUAL OILS FROM INK, SWEAT, OR DIRT SO A NEW COAT OF EMULSION WILL PROPERLY ADHERE TO THE SCREEN

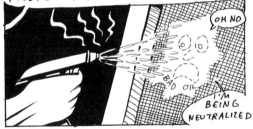

ALTHOUGH DEGREASER IS A POWERFUL SOLVENT, CAPABLE OF MAKING YOUR NOSE HAIRS FALL OUT AND ERADICATING YOUR OLFACTORY NERVES, IT'S REALLY IMPORTANT TO USE BECAUSE IT WILL ENSURE THE QUALITY OF FUTURE PRINTS

149

154

155

156

Yes,

"Do It Together Screenprinting" is the third issue in the "Do-It-Yourself Silkscreening" series. I think the name-change is appropriate for a few reasons:

① The first is that **Doing-It-Together** is at least as if not **more important** than **doing-it-yourself.** Not only can we accomplish more by sharing, listening, and learning, but we also have access to more resources, and use up less resources by sharing.

② The second reason is that **I really don't know** that much about screenprinting compared to an industry professional. This comic is about the summer I spent **learning from people** who know more about screenprinting than I do. Thanks Jon, Alethea, and Randy.

③ I want to acknowledge the **efforts of my peers** in the Do-It-Yourself movement who have remained critical of the ever-increasingly popular (and marketable) notion of **DIY.** My humble thanks go out to Rebecca Criscillis of the **Skullshare** Skillshare workshop, Karen Switzer of **Ker-bloom** zine, and the band **Takaru** for their song "Ringbearer". All of these **people have spoken** to me with their voices, writing, and music in a way that re-affirms my hesitation about constantly using a Do-It-Yourself approach for every problem or obstacle.

☆ It's interesting that when you begin to do things for yourself, you immediately realize the importance of **community.**

157

"Pinch" 2007 - screenprint ink on acrylic

SCREENPRINTER PROFILE: JONATHAN RUNCIO

What inspired you to start screen-printing?
Instant gratification.

What type of surfaces do you print on? (Paper - comic covers - posters - fine art / Fabric - Clothing - patches / Other materials - glass - wood...)
I've printed on it all. More posters and cd jackets than I can count. Currently printing on acrylic, bullet proof glass, vinyl, aluminum and t-shirts.

What types of ink do you use?
Plasitsols for t's. House paint for paper. Nazdar 9700 for everything else.

What size print runs do you do? (100's - 10's?)
With the majority of my art, I only print each stencil only once. The largest run I've printed was 3000 units for a Japanese music festival program.

How many colors do you generally use per design?
1- 15. No more

How do you separate and register colors? (on a computer - photoshop - illustrator / by hand with sharpie and vellum / with stencils)
I use Illustrator and sometimes Photoshop for seps. Then I use an Epson 3000, to print my films.

How do you protect yourself from toxic materials such as inks and solvents while printing / cleaning up?
I've just started using a respirator when printing with solvent based inks.

Where do you print?
A small room attached to the back of our house.

What do you listen to while you print?
Lately, Albert Ayler's box set, Reynols, Dead C, Shadow Ring, Intersystems, Angus Maclise, Vholtz, ESG. Plus, I make cd's of field recordings then scratch them up so they skip/loop. Never the same sounds. Inspiring.

Where can we see your work?
Ratio 3 in San Francisco in October. NADA in Miami in December. Also at www.runcio.com

PRINTING ON PAPER

CANDACE IS RIGHT ABOUT ALL THE TOXIC CHEMICALS USED IN PLASTISOL INKS AND IN T-SHIRT PRINTING SHOPS IN GENERAL— THAT'S WHY I LIKE PRINTING WITH WATER-BASED INKS

SCREEN

JIFFY HINGES

HALF-INCH THICK PLYWOOD

PAPER

VERSATEX
TOTALLY MEANT FOR PAPER ONLY

SCREEN PR
TRANSPAR
BASE MED

YOU CAN THIN DOWN OR EXTEND YOUR INKS WITH **TRANSPARENT BASE MEDIUMS**— DO NOT MIX MORE THAN ½ MEDIUM AND ½ INK

USE **CARDSTOCK PAPER**, CLASSIC CREST 100-POUND COVER STOCK, TWO-PLY HOT PRESS BRISTOL, OR SOME PAPER THICK ENOUGH TO ABSORB INK.

BOLT

NUT

CLAMPS

HINGE

SCREW

JIFFY HINGES ARE CLAMPS ON HINGES THAT ALLOW YOU TO RAISE AND LOWER THE SCREEN SO IT ALWAYS LANDS IN THE SAME PLACE. YOU CAN BUY THESE FOR $30 A PAIR AT ART STORES OR WWW.CREATIVESCREENTECH.COM

BY PRINTING ON PAPER YOU CAN CREATE VERY LARGE DESIGNS, LIKE EVENT POSTERS, OR VERY SMALL DESIGNS LIKE BUSINESS CARDS— USE 195 THREADS PER INCH MESH!

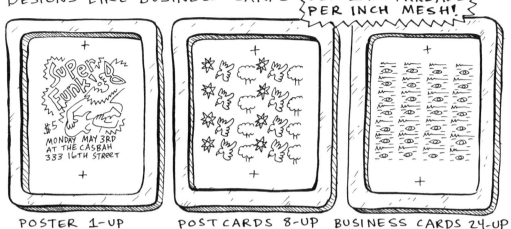

POSTER 1-UP   POST CARDS 8-UP   BUSINESS CARDS 24-UP

IN ORDER TO PRINT WITH MAXIMUM EFFICIENCY, YOU MUST "**MULTI-UP**" YOUR DESIGN, IF POSSIBLE

THIS SIMPLY MEANS PRINTING MULTIPLE IMAGES WITH ONE PASS OF THE SQUEEGEE

AND THEN CUTTING THESE MULTIPLE IMAGES DOWN TO SIZE:

1-UP

2-UP

THERE ARE A BUNCH OF WAYS TO **MULTI-UP** A DESIGN ON A FILM OR TRANSPARENCY BEFORE YOU BURN A SCREEN: EITHER USE SCISSORS AND TAPE AND A PHOTO-COPY MACHINE OR USE THE "**STEP-AND-REPEAT**" FUNCTION IN A COMPUTER PROGRAM LIKE QUARK OR INDESIGN

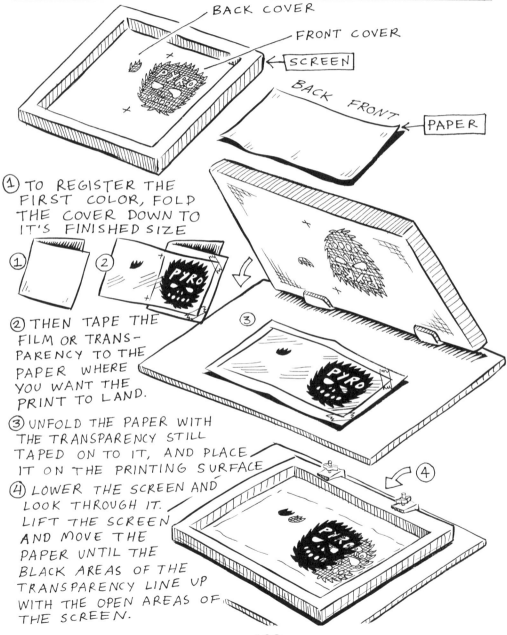

FOR PRINTING BOOK COVERS, COMPACT DISC COVERS, ENVELOPES, BOXES, PACKAGING, OR ANY PAPER THAT WILL BE FOLDED, IT'S A GOOD IDEA TO PRINT THE PAPER WHILE IT'S **STILL FLAT**

BACK COVER

FRONT COVER

SCREEN

BACK FRONT

PAPER

① TO REGISTER THE FIRST COLOR, FOLD THE COVER DOWN TO IT'S FINISHED SIZE

② THEN TAPE THE FILM OR TRANS-PARENCY TO THE PAPER WHERE YOU WANT THE PRINT TO LAND.

③ UNFOLD THE PAPER WITH THE TRANSPARENCY STILL TAPED ON TO IT, AND PLACE IT ON THE PRINTING SURFACE

④ LOWER THE SCREEN AND LOOK THROUGH IT. LIFT THE SCREEN AND MOVE THE PAPER UNTIL THE BLACK AREAS OF THE TRANSPARENCY LINE UP WITH THE OPEN AREAS OF THE SCREEN.

162

⑤ ONCE THE PAPER IS PLACED WHERE YOU WANT IT, YOU CAN USE REGISTRATION GUIDES TO MARK THAT SPOT. REGISTRATION GUIDES CAN BE PIECES OF TAPE, PHOTO CORNERS, OR A PENCIL MARK.

I RECOMMEND USING SEVERAL PIECES OF TAPE STACKED ON TOP OF EACH OTHER SO THE PAPER CAN BUTT UP AGAINST THE TAPE

TOP VIEW

USE SEVERAL STRIPS OF TAPE LAYERED ON TOP OF EACH OTHER

SIDE VIEW

ALWAYS USE THE **THREE-POINT REGISTRATION SYSTEM**: MARK WHERE THREE CORNERS OF THE PAPER SHOULD LAND

EXTRA-LONG TAPE = EXTRA SECURITY

FANCY PHOTO-CORNERS

WHEN YOU'RE READY TO PRINT BE SURE TO HAVE SOME NEWSPAPER NEARBY TO PUT DOWN YOUR INKY SQUEEGEE

PAPER STOCK, STACKED AND CLOSE AT HAND TO BE PRINTED ON

120 VOLT PHOTO-MEDIUM BEAM - 100 WATTS EXPOSES SCREEN: 4 MINUTES

PYRO

YOUR FIRST FEW PRINTS WILL **NOT** BE PERFECT - BE SURE YOU FLOOD THE SCREEN AND USE SCRATCH PAPER OR NEWSPRINT WHILE YOU MAKE ADJUSTMENTS

THE LOWER CLAMP WILL GIVE THE SCREEN A LITTLE BIT OF OFF-CONTACT

IF YOU NEED MORE OFF-CONTACT, YOU CAN TAPE A PIECE OF CARDBOARD TO THE FRAME UNDER THE SCREEN

ONCE YOU GET DECENT TEST PRINTS, START USING YOUR NICE PAPER

164

A WORD ABOUT INK: **INK LIKES TO STICK TO INK!** WHEN YOU PRINT, IF YOU ARE NOT USING A VACUUM TABLE, OR SPRAY ADHESIVE, THE PAPER WILL STICK TO THE BACK OF YOUR SCREEN:

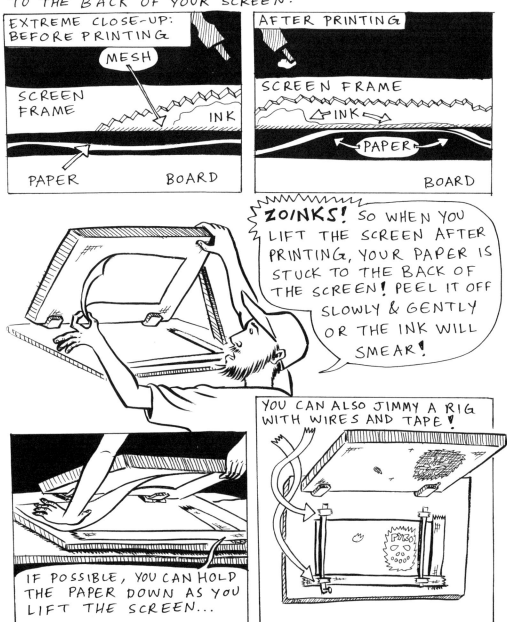

EXTREME CLOSE-UP: BEFORE PRINTING

MESH

SCREEN FRAME

INK

PAPER   BOARD

AFTER PRINTING

SCREEN FRAME

INK

PAPER

BOARD

ZOINKS! SO WHEN YOU LIFT THE SCREEN AFTER PRINTING, YOUR PAPER IS STUCK TO THE BACK OF THE SCREEN! PEEL IT OFF SLOWLY & GENTLY OR THE INK WILL SMEAR!

IF POSSIBLE, YOU CAN HOLD THE PAPER DOWN AS YOU LIFT THE SCREEN...

YOU CAN ALSO JIMMY A RIG WITH WIRES AND TAPE!

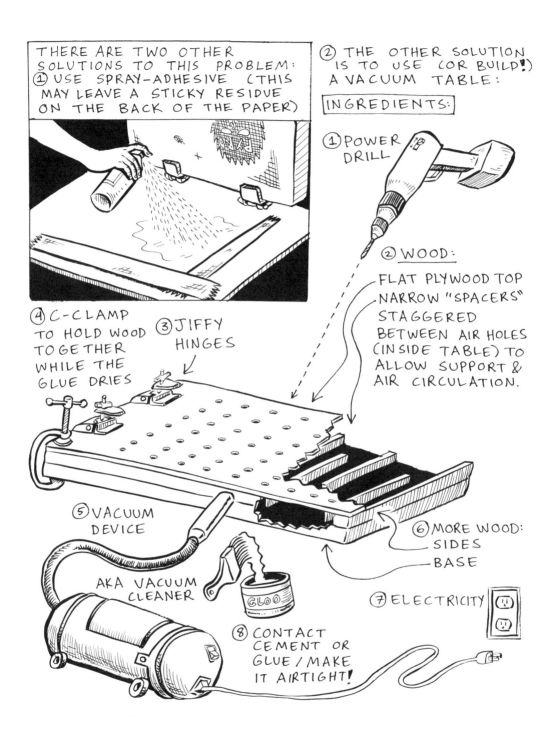

THERE ARE TWO OTHER SOLUTIONS TO THIS PROBLEM:
① USE SPRAY-ADHESIVE (THIS MAY LEAVE A STICKY RESIDUE ON THE BACK OF THE PAPER)

② THE OTHER SOLUTION IS TO USE (OR BUILD!) A VACUUM TABLE:

INGREDIENTS:

① POWER DRILL

② WOOD:
FLAT PLYWOOD TOP NARROW "SPACERS" STAGGERED BETWEEN AIR HOLES (INSIDE TABLE) TO ALLOW SUPPORT & AIR CIRCULATION.

④ C-CLAMP TO HOLD WOOD TOGETHER WHILE THE GLUE DRIES

③ JIFFY HINGES

⑤ VACUUM DEVICE

AKA VACUUM CLEANER

GLOO

⑥ MORE WOOD:
SIDES
BASE

⑦ ELECTRICITY

⑧ CONTACT CEMENT OR GLUE / MAKE IT AIRTIGHT!

ANOTHER PROBLEM WITH WATER-BASED INKS IS THAT, IF THEY SIT FOR TOO LONG IN YOUR SCREEN, THEY WILL DRY, FILLING IN DETAIL AND GIVING YOU CRAPPY PRINTS!

WTF?

FOR THIS REASON, IT IS IMPORTANT TO NOT STOP PRINTING ONCE YOU START

GUESS I SHOULDN'T HAVE STOPPED TO MAKE LUNCH—

BURP!

IF THE INK BEGINS TO DRY WHILE YOU ARE PRINTING, SPRAY A MIXTURE OF 20% SCREEN CLEANER (OR 409 FANTASTIC CLEANER) AND 80% WATER ON THE ENTIRE SCREEN.

20% 409

80% WATER

IF YOU DO THIS, THE INK WILL BE A LITTLE RUNNY, SO PRINT WITH A FEW TEST SHEETS AFTERWARDS

CAP'N CRUNCH! SAVE ME FROM THE SOG MONSTER!

THE TRANSPARENT BASE MEDIUM YOU MIX WITH THE INK ACTS AS AN EXTENDER AND RETARDER, WHICH SLOWS THE DRYING SPEED OF THE INK

+ INK = MAGIC INK!

YOU CAN ALSO PRINT WITH ACRYLIC PAINT, HOUSE PAINT, OR WHATEVER A SQUEEGEE CAN PUSH THROUGH A SCREEN! JUST MIX IT WITH THE RIGHT MEDIUM TO KEEP IT FROM DRYING TOO FAST!

I'M OUTTA RED—TIME TO BREAK OUT THE KETCHUP!

WHEN YOU ARE DONE PRINTING YOUR FIRST COLOR, WASH OUT THE SCREEN AND STACK THE DRY PRINTS - PUT THEM UNDER SOMETHING HEAVY TO MINIMIZE BUCKLING!

I CHING
OVID
ANVIL
PRINTS

REMOVE THE OLD REGISTRATION GUIDES AND ATTACH THE SCREEN FOR THE SECOND COLOR:

TAPE A PIECE OF MYLAR* DOWN WHERE THE PRINT WILL LAND BUT PUT THE TAPE OUTSIDE OF WHERE THE SCREEN WILL LAND.

TAPE BEYOND SCREEN-LANDING ZONE

SCREEN WILL LAND HERE

PRINT THE SECOND COLOR ON THE MYLAR

THEN SLIDE ONE OF THE PRINTS OF THE FIRST COLOR UNDER THE MYLAR AND LINE IT UP TO THE PRINT OF THE SECOND COLOR

ONCE THE PRINT IS LINED UP TO THE MYLAR...

EUREKA!

CAREFULLY LIFT THE MYLAR WITHOUT MOVING THE PRINT...

...AND PUT DOWN NEW REGISTRATION MARKS

NOW YOU CAN PRINT YOUR SECOND COLOR!

WATER-BASED INKS ARE TRANSPARENT: THE COLOR OF THE PAPER SHOWS THROUGH THEM & WHEN TWO COLORS OF INK OVERLAP, THEY CREATE A THIRD COLOR

IF YOU DON'T WANT TO USE MYLAR, YOU CAN ALSO REGISTER COLORS BY TAPING THE TRANSPARENCY OF THE SECOND COLOR TO A PRINT OF THE FIRST COLOR AND LOOKING THROUGH THE SCREEN

IF YOU DON'T WANT TO DEAL WITH COLOR REGISTRATION AT ALL, YOU CAN CREATE A DESIGN THAT DOESN'T REQUIRE TIGHT COLOR REGISTRATION ~ FOR EXAMPLE, A DESIGN WITH NO OUTLINES, AND WITH NO COLORS THAT TOUCH EDGE-TO-EDGE:

IF YOUR PRINTS LOOK BLURRY THERE IS TOO MUCH INK GOING THROGH YOUR SCREEN.

YOU SHOULD EITHER ① USE A HARDER SQUEEGEE OR ② INCREASE THE OFF-CONTACT DISTANCE BETWEEN YOUR SCREEN AND SUBSTRATE BY TAPING A PIECE OF CARDBOARD TO THE BACK OF YOUR SCREEN:

BEFORE: BAD

AFTER: GOOD

REMEMBER: INK LIKES TO STICK TO INK! IF YOU HAVE NO OFF-CONTACT, WHEN YOU LIFT YOUR SCREEN AFTER PRINTING...

... THE INK YOU PRINTED ON YOUR SUBSTRATE WILL PULL EXCESS INK THROUGH YOUR SCREEN

DEATH CAB FOR CUTIE

FALL TOUR 2004

SCREENPRINTER PROFILE: JASON MUNN

What inspired you to start screen-printing?

I loved the idea of designing or illustrating something and doing the printing myself. Most of my time is spend in front of the computer so the printing is a great way to get my hands dirty again, so to speak.

What type of surfaces do you print on? (Paper - comic covers - posters - fine art / Fabric - Clothing - patches / Other materials - glass - wood...)

I've mostly just printed on paper.

What types of ink do you use?

I use Speedball permanent acrylic ink.

What size print runs do you do?

In most cases my print runs are between 100 - 200, although tour posters can go a little or a lot higher.

How many colors do you generally use per design?

I usually use two or three colors. I think I've only done one four color poster.

How do you separate and register colors? (on a computer - photoshop - illustrator / by hand with sharpie and vellum / with stencils)

I do most of my layout and design in Illustrator so this is also how I separate my colors. Putting each color on it's own layer and outputting them.

How do you protect yourself from toxic materials such as inks and solvents while printing / cleaning up?

The Speedball ink is non toxic and washes out with water. I like the feel of the Speedball ink, the non toxic aspect is a nice bonus as well.

Where do you print?

I print from a studio called Bloom Screen Printing in Oakland, CA. It's a one man print shop run by my friend Nat Swope. He also prints some of my larger run posters. We've done quite a few projects where I've done the design and he has done the printing.

What do you listen to while you print? (bands / talk radio / silence / birds/ hip hop / thrash??)

It always varies, but looking through my posters you would get a pretty good idea of my record collection. Also a lot of NPR while I'm printing.

Where can we see your work?

Various store windows before the shows and www.thesmallstakes.com after the shows.

173

MANUAL COLOR SEPARATIONS

THIS IS HOW YOU CAN CREATE TRANSPARENCIES OF ADDITIONAL COLORS WITHOUT ANY FANCY COMPUTER SHENANIGANS:

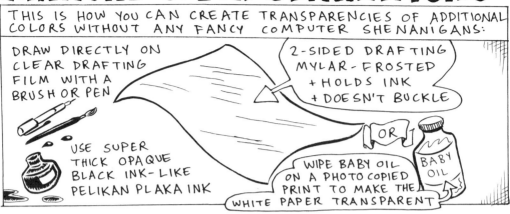

DRAW DIRECTLY ON CLEAR DRAFTING FILM WITH A BRUSH OR PEN

USE SUPER THICK OPAQUE BLACK INK-LIKE PELIKAN PLAKA INK

2-SIDED DRAFTING MYLAR-FROSTED
+ HOLDS INK
+ DOESN'T BUCKLE

OR

BABY OIL

WIPE BABY OIL ON A PHOTOCOPIED PRINT TO MAKE THE WHITE PAPER TRANSPARENT

TAPE YOUR FIRST DRAWING TO A LIGHTBOX OR A WINDOW (IF IT'S SUNNY OUTSIDE), THEN TAPE ANOTHER PIECE OF DRAFTING FILM OR PAPER OVER THAT. FILL IN OR DRAW WHERE YOU WANT ADDITIONAL COLORS TO GO

USE A NEW SHEET OF DRAFTING FILM FOR EACH COLOR YOU WANT TO ADD. YOU CAN BURN A SCREEN USING THE DRAFTING FILM AS A TRANSPARENCY.

LIGHT BOX

ORIGINAL DRAWING (OUTLINE)

SECOND COLOR FILL-IN - THIS WILL BE PRINTED FIRST, AND THE OUTLINE SECOND

CUTTING STENCILS BY HAND

WHAT IF YOU JUST RAN OUT OF EMULSION, OR YOU HAVE A REALLY SIMPLE DESIGN?

WHAT IF IT'S THE APOCALYPSE OR A NUCLEAR WINTER AND THERE'S NO ELECTRICITY OR SUNLIGHT TO BURN SCREENS? WHAT THEN

FOR SCREENPRINTING, I RECOMMEND USING VERY THIN .003 MYLAR

IT IS STRONG AND DURABLE, YET EASY TO CUT.

THIS MAKES IT REALLY EASY TO PRINT BECAUSE EVERY TIME YOU LIFT YOUR SCREEN, THE STENCIL COMES WITH IT.

WOULD THAT STOP YOU FROM SCREENPRINTING? OF COURSE NOT!

BRIDGE

ISLAND

OLD SC

YOU COULD ALWAYS ROLL REAL OLD SCHOOL STYLE AND CUT A STENCIL

IT IS SO THIN THAT IT HOLDS A SMALL STATIC ELECTRICITY CHARGE WHICH MAKES IT STICK TO YOUR SCREEN!

IF THERE IS NO ADHESIVE OR ELECTRICAL CHARGE, THE INK WILL USUALLY MAKE THE STENCIL STICK TO THE SCREEN...

WHOOPS

...USUALLY...

SQUEEGIE MOVES

ASIDE OF THE COMMONLY USED FLOOD AND PRINT STROKES (MENTIONED EARLIER) THERE IS A WIDE VARIETY OF SQUEEGIE MOVES & TECHNIQUES:

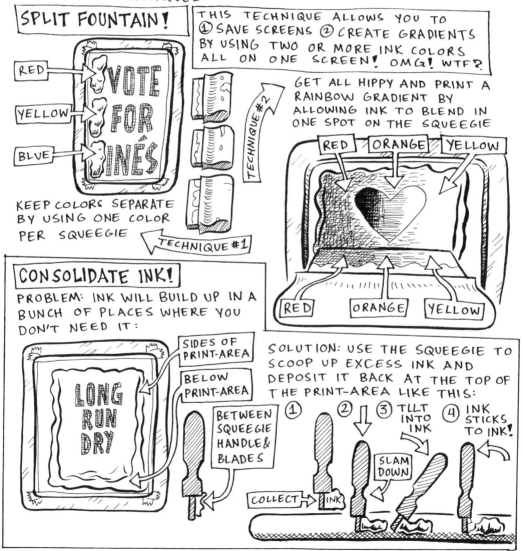

SPLIT FOUNTAIN!

RED

YELLOW

BLUE

VOTE FOR ~~LINES~~

KEEP COLORS SEPARATE BY USING ONE COLOR PER SQUEEGIE

TECHNIQUE #1

TECHNIQUE #2

THIS TECHNIQUE ALLOWS YOU TO ① SAVE SCREENS ② CREATE GRADIENTS BY USING TWO OR MORE INK COLORS ALL ON ONE SCREEN! OMG! WTF?

GET ALL HIPPY AND PRINT A RAINBOW GRADIENT BY ALLOWING INK TO BLEND IN ONE SPOT ON THE SQUEEGIE

RED   ORANGE   YELLOW

RED   ORANGE   YELLOW

CONSOLIDATE INK!

PROBLEM: INK WILL BUILD UP IN A BUNCH OF PLACES WHERE YOU DON'T NEED IT:

LONG RUN DRY

SIDES OF PRINT-AREA

BELOW PRINT-AREA

BETWEEN SQUEEGIE HANDLE & BLADES

SOLUTION: USE THE SQUEEGIE TO SCOOP UP EXCESS INK AND DEPOSIT IT BACK AT THE TOP OF THE PRINT-AREA LIKE THIS:

① ② ③ TLLT INTO INK ④ INK STICKS TO INK!

SLAM DOWN

COLLECT → INK

Screenprinting
Today: The Basics

by Andy MacDougall

ISBN: 0-9739001-0-5

Stencil Pirates by Josh MacPhee
ISBN: 1-9329360-15-8   Soft Skull Press

The Gospel of Screenprinting by Brad Bane
Ten-forty-five press
available from www.cutxpaste.com or www.etsy.com

"Choosing the right squeegie" by Terry Combs
available on-line at screenprinters.net/articles.php

Healing with Whole Foods by Paul Pitchford
ISBN: 978-1556434303

"African Screenprinting: Harare's Unsung Type Heroes"
by Saki Mafundikwa
Eye magazine 59 vol.15 Spring 2006

How to Screen Print the Adventure Land Way
a skillshare by Heather Q
Welcometoadventureland.com

FIGHT FOR YOUR HOME

LUCHA PARA SU HOGAR

EVICTION DEFENSE COLLABORATIVE 431-8831 • HOUSING RIGHTS COMMITTEE 703-8644

SCREENPRINTER PROFILE:
SAN FRANCISCO SCREENPRINTING COLLECTIVE

What inspired you to start screen-printing ?

The SFPC is a printmaking collective that uses graphic art to support social justice organizing. The SFPC started in February of the year 2000 when a group of silkscreen artists met at Mission Grafika, a community-based, non-profit printshop. We came together to make posters collectively, and our first campaign addressed the impact of gentrification in the Mission District. After our first project we joined an anti-displacement coalition and built close ties to housing groups who serve low income, immigrant communities. Taking inspiration from the Chicano Poster Movement and San Francisco's rich history of political graphics, we make public art to challenge the mass media and broadcast progressive politics directly to the streets.

What type of surfaces do you print on?

The SFPC primarily prints posters on paper for use in community outreach and political demonstrations. We have also printed on wood, armbands, banners and canvas for some of our past campaigns.

What types of ink do you use?

Water based ink.

What size print runs do you do?

As low as 10 and as high as 1000 depending on the campaign.

How many colors do you generally use per design?

Limited colors usually 1, 2 or 3 to allow for higher print runs.

How do you separate and register colors?

Primarily with computer programs.

How do you protect yourself from toxic materials such as inks and solvents while printing / cleaning up?

Use water based ink. Also use latex gloves, air circulation and extraction fans.

Where do you print?

At the homes of our members, in non profit print studios and in local galleries.

Where can we see your work?

Primarily on the streets of SF. Our website is sfprintcollective.com

What is the social or political importance of screenprinting to you?

The SFPC supports progressive community organizing through grass-roots media campaigns, street level posters and silkscreen classes. Our politics are internationalist, but our focus is on local issues, such as housing and homelessness, that affect people's daily lives. We believe political power comes from the grassroots through direct action, and we see elections as a potential tactic to defend our rights. We want direct, democratic control for our communities, and we envision a future without capitalism where human needs come before corporate greed.

Contact the SFPC at sfprintcollective@gmail.com

GLOSSARY of TERMS

SOME OF THESE DEFINITIONS ARE STOLEN FROM WWW.WIKIPEDIA.COM AND SOME I WROTE MYSELF. SEE IF YOU CAN TELL WHICH IS WHICH!

Acetate- A clear sheet of vellum or paper that can be used as a transparency for exposing screens when drawn on directly with black opaque ink.

Back-white- Layer of white ink, usually on dyed fabrics, over which other colors of ink are printed for higher contrast-value.

Blow-out gun- Gun that shoots a high-pressure spray of solvent powerful enough to remove unwanted spots of cured ink.

"Burning a screen" - See Exposing a screen

Carousel Press- A t-shirt press with pallets and screen clamps that rotate independently on a central axis.

Coating a screen - Covering the mesh on a screen with a thin, even layer of emulsion.

Color separations- Dividing an image by color and creating one new image per color, consisting only of that color, so that when all the separations overlap, the original image is re-created.

Conveyor Dryer- An industrail dryer used for curing inks once they are printed on fabric. A conveyor belt runs through the dryer for continuous production.

Cure- A chemical change that hardens and permanently bonds an ink to its substrate

Dark room - A room for storing light-sensitive chemicals.

Degreaser - Highly toxic solvent used for removing oil, dust, grease, and dirt.

CMYK- Cyan, Magenta, Yellow, Keyline (or Black) This is also known as **Subtractive Color** which explains the theory of mixing paints, dyes, inks, and natural colorants to create colors which absorb some wavelengths of light and reflect others.

DPI - Dots per Inch is a measure of printing resolution, in particular the number of individual dots of ink a printer or toner can produce within a linear one-inch (2.54 cm) space

Emulsion - A mixture of two immiscible (unblendable) substances. One substance (the dispersed phase) is dispersed in the other (the continuous phase).

180

Durometer – One of several ways to indicate the hardness of a material, defined as the material's resistance to permanent indentation.

Frame – Rigid bars, usually made of wood or aluminum, on which the screen mesh is tightly stretched.

Emulsion Coater – A small hand-held metal trough that holds photo-emulsion for the purpose of evenly coating the screen.

Exposing a screen – The process of exposing a screen covered by a dry coat of photo-emulsion to a light source for a specific amount of time. Exposure causes a chemical change in the light-sensitive particles. These particles harden, thus closing off the mesh in that part of the screen. Areas of the emulsion protected from exposure do not undergo this change and are later washed-out, leaving the screen mesh open for ink to pass through.

Exposure unit – Usually a piece of glass or plexi-glass and a table that holds the film, transparency, or stencil in contact with the emulsion on the screen while it is exposed to a light source (also part of the exposure unit). Most exposure units include a timer and vacuum-seal.

Films – Flexible, transparent sheets of polyester, plastic, or celluloid that can hold an image made of ink or toner.

Flash-dryer – A small, moveable dryer, usually mounted on small wheels, with a stand that allows it to rest over a flat surface such as a table or platen on a carousel press.

Flood-Stroke – The squeegie stroke that covers the image-area with ink, so that each open area of mesh has ink above it and is primed to print

Gradient – Gradual change over distance from one color to another

Gutter – Area along inside edge of screen where mesh meets frame.

Halide – Metal-halides are high-intensity discharge lamps, such as those used in modern street lights.

Illustrator – Adobe Illustrator is a vector-based drawing computer program designed and marketted by Adobe Systems.

LPI - Lines per Inch is a measurement of printing resolution in systems that use a half tone screen. Specifically it is a measure of how close together the lines in the halftone grid are.

Mesh- Criss-crossing nylon threads stretched on a frame. Ink passes between the threads to make a print on a substrate. Mesh can be either very wide or very fine to let more or less ink through.

Mineral Spirits- Mineral Spirits is a petroleum distillate commonly used as a paint thinner and mild solvent.

Mylar- Biaxially-oriented polyethylene terephthalate (boPET) polyester film is used for its high tensile strength, chemical and dimensional stability, transparency, gas and aroma barrier properties and electrical insulation. boPET film withstands high heat and is often used as overhead transparency film for photocopiers or laser printer.

Newtons - The Newton is the international unit of force. It is named after Isaac Newton in recognition of his work in classical mechanics. One newton is the force of Earth's gravity on an apple with a mass of about 102 grams.

Off-contact - The distance between the bottom-side of the screen and the substrate before and after the print is made.

Pallet (or Platen) - The hard flat surface that supports the substrate and holds it in place during printing.

Pantone- Pantone Inc. is a corporation headquartered in Carlstadt, New Jersey. The company is best known for it's Pantone Matching System (PMS), a proprietary space used in a variety of industries, primarily printing, though sometimes in the manufacture of colored paint, fabric, and plastics.

Pelon- A soft, flat piece of fabric designed not to stick to other fabrics. Often used to make test prints onto.

Photo-emulsion - A photo-sensitive substance that hardens when subjected to ultra-violet light.

Photoshop- A graphics editting computer program designed and marketted by Adobe Systems.

Pinhole - A tiny hole in the emulsion a screen.

Pixelation- In computer graphics, pixellation is an effect caused by displaying a bitmap at such a large size that individual pixels, small single-colored square display elements, are visible to the naked eye.

PPI - Pixels per Inch or pixel density is a measurement of a computer display's resolution, related to the size of the display in inches and the total number of pixels in the horizontal and vertical directions.

Process color - A shortened form of the term "Four-color printing process" which refers to the method of reproducing color on a printing press

Raster - A raster graphics image, digital image, or bitmap is a computer data file representing a rectangular grid of pixels, or points of color on a computer monitor, paper, or other display medium.

Reclaimer - An extremely toxic solvent used to strip hardened emulsion from a screen, so that the screen may be re-coated and burned with a different image.

RGB - Red Green Blue or an additive color system involves light emitted directly from a source or illuminant such as light blub, TV monitor, traffic light, or computer monitor.

Registration - Alignment of different prints on a surface. Especially relevant in four-color process CMYK, or spot color printing because colors are separated onto plates or screens and then re-aligned to register accurately on a substrate.

Scanner - General-purpose device which digitizes a two-dimensional image.

Sensitizer - Light-sensitive particle suspended in 2-part emulsion

Squeegie - Rubber straight edge with a handle for pushing ink through a screen using a continuous even pressure.

Split-Fountain - Using several colors of ink on a single screen to either create gradients, conserve screens, or print multiple colors with a single screen.

Spot colors - In offset printing, a spot color is any color generated by an ink (pure or mixed) that is printed using a single run.

Stencil - A template used to draw, paint, or print identical letters, symbols, or images every time it is used. Stencils are formed by removing sections from a template material in the form of text or an image.

Substrate - The base material that images will be printed onto.

Three-point registration - Markings on a pallet or printing surface where three corners of a sheet of paper should land. Ensures that each substrate recieves a print in the exact same location.

Tape-out - Process of closing off open sections of the screen

Toner - A powder used in laser printers and photocopiers to form text and images.

Transparency - A thin sheet of transparent, flexible material, typically celluloid, on to which figures can be drawn.

Trapping - In the color-separation phase of pre-press, trapping consists of creating small overlaps between abutting colors in order to mask color registration problems.

T-square - A technical drawing instrument used for drawing horizontal lines on a drafting table.

Vector - Vector graphics is the use of geometrical primitives such as points, lines, curves, and polygons, which are all based on mathematical equations to represent images in computer graphics.

Wash-out - Process of washing unexposed emulsion out of a screen that has been exposed to light

Wet-on-wet - Printing one color of ink over another before the first print has dried

Xylene - A solvent used in the printing, rubber, and leather industries. Xylene affects the brain. It can cause unconsciousness and even death at high levels. Xylene is also used in art supplies like pens, and other writing and drawing tools.

THANK YOU: Joe Biel and all at microcosm, Age Scott, Larry Brown, Tom Isaacson, Holly, Mom, Dad, and Beste. Jonathan Runcio, Randy Lee, Dave Schwartz, Andy Hartzell, Jesse Reklaw, Shannon O'Leary, Geoff Vasile, Jared Katz, Anna Brown, Becca Criscillis, Emily Cohen, Ben Coleman, Josh MacPhee, Joe Sayers, Erin Allard, Josh Rosenstock, Sara Tolley, Jose Guinto, Mark Haven Britt, Isla Prieto, Carla Costa, Tim Rogers, Suzanne Husky, Taylor Neaman, Nate Beaty, Daria Tessler, Ananda Kessler, Jason Munn, Hot Iron Press, SF Print Collective, Monica Canilao, Dirty drawers, Creative Screen Tech, Artist & Craftsman Supply, SF Zine Fest and Portland Zine Symposium organizers & attendees!

ARTISTS

www.animalsleepstories.com
www.thesmallstakes.com
www.runcio.com
www.taylormadeclothes.com
www.sfprintcollective.com
www.monicacanilao.com
www.hotironpress.com

SUPPLIES

www.creativescreentech.com
www.nazdar.com
www.silkscreensupplies.com
www.screenprinters.net
www.tmiscreenprinting.com
www.ryanrss.com
www.revels.com
www.midwestsignandscreen.com

MORE

www.justseeds.org
www.nomediakings.org
www.dieselfuelprints.com
www.gigposters.com
www.threadless.com
www.stencilarchive.org
www.seripop.com
www.ryanmcginness.com
www.cellspace.org
www.missionculturalcenter.org
www.space1026.com
www.rpscollective.com
www.usscatastrophe/
zettwoch/silkscreen.html

JOHN ISAACSON lives in Portland, OR and was born in Santa Barbara on the cusp of Taurus and Aries in the year 1976. He writes and draws the comics Do-It-Yourself Screenprinting, Pyromania, and Feedback. For six years, he taught after-school cartooning classes in the Bay Area. He now teaches after school programs in Portland.

You can see more of his artwork and t-shirts on the opposite page or at www.unlay.com

www.unlay.com